At the Redemption Center

At the Redemption Center

Poems by

Anne Sandor

© 2026 Anne Sandor. All rights reserved.
This material may not be reproduced in any form, published,
reprinted, recorded, performed, broadcast,
rewritten or redistributed without
the explicit permission of Anne Sandor.
All such actions are strictly prohibited by law.

Cover design by Shay Culligan
Cover image by Nitrub on iStock
Author photo by Jennifer Davis Photography

ISBN: 978-1-63980-817-5

Kelsay Books
502 South 1040 East, A-119
American Fork, Utah 84003
Kelsaybooks.com

For my mother, Athena.

Acknowledgments

Thank you to the following publications, in which versions of these poems previously appeared:

823 on High: "What Boys Fear," "The Truth About Prodigals," "Alchemy"

Allen Ginsberg Poetry Awards, *Paterson Literary Review:* "Mirror Writing"

Strange Fruit: Poems on the Death Penalty: "The Last Supper"

Contents

At the Redemption Center	13
Wishbone	14
What Boys Fear	15
There Is Always a Girl in a Box	16
Motown	17
Flash Art	18
Pantoum for My Granddaughter	20
Mickey Mousing in Bliss Park	21
A Balancing Act	23
The Veneration of Mothers	24
Mirror Writing	26
The Dutch Door	28
The Truth About Prodigals	29
What Endures	30
Adult Home	31
The Family Tree	32
Ossuaries	34
The Perspective from Blue Bridge	36
Detritus at the US-Mexican Border	40
Citizens of Paradise: Jay Austin and Lauren Geoghegan	41
What Heather Heyer's Mom Wants	42
Queers	43
The Pillars of Evolution	45
Branding	48
The Last Supper	50
At the Bird Feeder	52
Ibis	53
Alchemy	54
How to Eat at a Civilized Table	56
A Tale of Two Falafels	57

A Family Outing in Harriman State Park	58
In the Dark of Night	59
Yes, I Talk Too Much	62
Soft Power	65

At the Redemption Center

At the redemption center
you bring the empty vessels,
the washed, the unwashed,
and sort them by kind.

Though all yield the same return,
the clean and the foul,
each rendered by what can be
burned or saved, purified or extracted,

you hope with each offering
for the redemption of us all.

Wishbone

The coveted wishbone
you and your brother fought over,
a sticky end tight in your fist,
the savage play for a wish come true,
and his face in that moment,
before you let go, desperate.

What Boys Fear

New first graders, my grandson and his friends
are busy becoming men, scaring
themselves in every imaginable way.

He comes home asking about serial killers,
whispering the words as if sharing
a secret to gauge our reaction.

He doesn't want his mother to walk the dog
late at night, afraid Butchy will drag her
off into the woods, lose her in the dark.

He wants to know if earthquakes can strike,
how bad they will be, and what about
waterspouts, though we live far from any ocean.

His voice at these times is neutral, he's just
making an inquiry and not terrified,
but his wary eyes say otherwise.

He mistakes meanness for strength,
practices on his little sister,
who adores and forgives him.

So when he decides to be the Grim Reaper
for Halloween, I ask him why and he says,
Because he's scary, with his best brave face.

He wants to put on the mask,
carry the scythe, develop a thick skin
that will carry him through this world,
believes his life depends on this.

There Is Always a Girl in a Box

Some men like their girls in giant cake-
shaped boxes, slathered with whipped cream,
to pop out singing sweetly in swimwear,

while husbands keep theirs in pumpkin shells
because having wooed them,
they lack the wit and charm to keep them,

and fearful mothers prefer locking daughters
in a room—preferably atop a tower,
never to emerge, marry, grow disillusioned.

Magicians like women in boxes
they can saw in half, then magically restore
to great fanfare: one, two, three . . . poof!

But my favorite is the girl who climbs in
of her own volition, cocks her hip and smiles
invitingly before shimmying down,

arms extended above her head, slowly disappearing,
unhinging her hips, her arm sockets, folding
herself like a fan, as we watch with bated breath,

wait for it, the big reveal as he flips the lid open,
and we find her gone, out of the box for good.

Motown

Lined-up in the Wilson's basement
on a Saturday night, we'd lip-synch
our way through the Supremes—
cooing, oohing, *Baby, baby*
where did our love go?

We craved that beehive, the sparkly earrings,
the spangly gowns slit up the side
and their long, graceful, grateful arms,
so inviting, hugging at just the right moment
their bare shoulders, their lonely selves.

Six Irish girls from Brooklyn,
miles from Motown,
no geography for how love works,
we wondered what kind of men could
abuse them and refuse them.

We let the weight of our skinny arms
and this new girl-faith sway us, syncopated
hips sashaying in time, waiting open-
armed for our hearts to break,
dreaming of the songs we would sing.

Flash Art

The dark pink peony and the drowsy bee,
an emerald snake coiled tighter than a fist,

Celtic knots, Sailor Jerry flash: bluebirds,
hearts, ribbons, anchors and tanks

lining the walls, a feast for the eyes,
but she knows what she wants.

There's not a moment under the needle
when she isn't aware of herself, the single

bright light overhead, the man
marking the cleft between her breasts.

She finds this delicious. The ability to commit,
a message she's willing to stand by for life.

There's a moment when she's afraid to look,
afraid she'll change her mind *now,*

but she loves the stain of the blue-black ink,
the burning prick of the needle,

the thickness and thinness of certain lines,
the way they cross one another.

It's her name in Korean and she can't help
but think of the possibilities this presents,

the various translations,
and what will be lost in them.

Pantoum for My Granddaughter

The note made clear her displeasure:
Some one nos how to ruin a girls day,
though at six all it takes is being told
to behave like a girl, act like a lady.

Some one knows how to ruin a girls day,
calling out as she's cartwheeling,
behave like a girl, act like a lady,
watching her brother spin clear ahead.

Calling out as she's cartwheeling,
someone knows how to ruin a girls day,
watching her brother spin clear ahead,
she heaves over bent knees, catching her breath.

Someone knows how to ruin a girl's day
even at twenty, and smart as a whip,
as she heaves over bent knees, catching her breath,
no longer listening, sure that good girl is dead.

Mickey Mousing in Bliss Park

Mickey Mousing,
the syncing
of music & movement,
think *Fantasia,*
a symphony & a mouse,

an orchestral crescendo
now matched to the arch
of a young boy's back
as he summersaults
off a skateboard,

the lo o o ong slide
of a trombone
perfectly pitched
as he grinds
alo o o ong a rail,

the plucking
of a harp as he
ollies and nollies
the board this way
and that,

the counterpoint
of flute one and flute two
and the slalom
through halfpipes,

the heavy,
bass chugging
of the tuba
as he pumps
his way home.

A Balancing Act

An equation, perhaps, could explain
how his one hand, palm heavenward,
could hold snug and steady the tiny feet
in patent leather Maryjanes, his daughter
aloft, arms thrown wide, her reckless
laughter pealing like a church bell.

Maybe his adolescent interest
in juggling can account for the grace
of one arm tucked behind his back,
the other cocked like a waiter's,
the better to serve up his sweet girl
in her flowery new dress.

But no need for wonder, the moment
he stops the slight bob and weave,
counterpoint to her sway, as she responds,
grows still, arms outstretched, the two
perfectly aligned, here is a trust you hope
keeps them steady all their lives.

The Veneration of Mothers

This Mother's Day I owe you
an apology, my children
who did not ask to be born.

What were we thinking,
your father and me,
newlyweds, imagining
the spectacular
fusion of our DNA,
that you would thank us
for making your lives possible?

What joy in a childhood
with only a few brilliant years
to know nothing, spend
an entire day on your back
in the green fragrant grass,
the sky a preposterous blue,
and every cloud imaginable.

Time would be better spent,
we thought, nailing those SATs,
memorizing the periodic table
while bussing tables, managing
a weekly wage, all in service
of that spectacular DNA.

Loving parents—
what could be worse?
Still, I hope you enjoy
this life you did not ask for,
wish for you now whatever
it is that makes you smile.

Mirror Writing

My mother is of that generation
when penmanship mattered,
a disciple of the Palmer method,
for which she won an award
recognizing her perfectly pitched slant,
the matched humps of her *M*s
and delicate curlicues crowning her *P*s,
the neatly aligned margins
and hyphens in all the right places.

Did she practice the names of boys
her immigrant parents would never
let her date, careers she could not pursue?
She often wrote with a steady hand
business letters for her father,
and for her illiterate mother, it was lists—
rice, milk, bread, to hold next to labels
while trolling the A&P aisles.

She became the mother
who persecuted her firstborn
over homework, repositioning my hands
on the paper and pen until I caved,
wrote in cursive worthy
of Catholic nuns—the only ones
who prized penmanship as much as she.

Bless her, bless them all,
but I wanted more than anything
my mother's knack
for mirror writing, a pen in each hand
poised in the center of the page,
shimmying further apart
in syncopated coordination
like Rogers and Astaire drifting
across a ballroom floor.
That was the perfect illustration
of her adaptation after a broken arm,
the first of many adjustments
in which she learned to become the girl
her parents prized, the one with a parlor trick
and beautiful handwriting,
her name pitched perfectly
in either direction.

The Dutch Door

Opening onto the broad-shouldered yard of our old house,
the dark green Dutch door my mother never got over,

not the surprise he'd made of it for her birthday,
nor the ease with which she could sample weather.

In summer it was the very thing to keep us children
out, but still within her fearsome earshot.

From this door-like-a-window, she could take
in the garden where fist-sized marigolds flowered

in the unlikeliest of neighborhoods, between
sandy beach and steep-set cliffs, in the smack

of sea salt and curling winds. You have to
understand how a woman could spend all day

at a sink or a stove, talking to herself or the dog,
in a green-sprigged apron dawn to dusk.

Then you would know there was no getting over,
that for her there could only be just the one house

and a back door that felt like the only door,
or not a door at all, but a window she could look out of.

The Truth About Prodigals

Let's not talk about the ones that got away,
the prodigal son run off with the circus,
the prodigal daughter not far behind,
off squandering their good fortunes,
your patience, love, money, what good
looks they'd got, their health,
the kindness of others.

Should they return, open your arms,
proclaim the miracle.

Let's talk about the ones who stayed
because you raised them so well:
the bitter son, the defeated daughter,
on whom nothing has been lavished,
not good looks, nor good fortune,
or a kind word, who gave up
families of their own to tend
your house, your needs.

Is it enough to tell them *take heart*
in having made safe choices, lived life
frugally, taken such small consolation?

So many sad stories,
but in the end the saddest of all,
with your dying breath, all you will
think of are the ones that got away;
and for the stalwart children,
a bitter pill to wonder no matter
how worthwhile their endeavors,
whether you could love them as much.

What Endures

At the end of the very long day,
lined up in recliners,
strapped in for sundown
—the crazy hour,
Flo's despair begins.

Not for the spouse outlived,
the fleeting pleasure of children
born and raised,
careers she did or did not have,

but for her father crawling home
from King's Bar
through the neighbor's hedge
stinking of sours and mean,

for her mother, her worry
a rope she hung herself with
every time he came home,

and the brothers she helped raise
while planning an escape
with a husband
she could only dream of.

Adult Home

In the adult home where we put my mother,
there are no restraints binding her to a bed or chair,
no lamb's wool posies or vests with thick straps.

The adults are free to roam at will, encouraged
to visit the large-print library, the craft room,
the kitchen with a working stove for tea or coffee.

There's a hairdresser and a laundry room
for those who still worry over nylon in the dryer,
prefer to hang unmentionables in the bathroom.

The carpet, the sofas and wing chairs, the wallpaper,
coordinated with the drapes. Linen tablecloths
in the dining room, ice cream for dessert.

What was she thinking when she said she'd rather be dead
than sit before the theater-sized television
showing every movie made in the 40s & 50s,

movies we watched together on the *Late Show*
and the *Late Late Show,* only here, it's afternoon
and there's a cart with tea and cookies.

What's not to love about heat set at 90 degrees year round
or the aides, young and cheerful even on bath days?
Birds in cages trilling from every nook and cranny?

I could sit here on the sofa all day, nestled between Harry,
who's promised to show me how to parachute jump, and Ada,
who smiles a lot and wrings her hands.

The Family Tree

I.

Leaf by leaf my husband is replacing the fallen.

In the cellar he excavates photographs,
letters as fine as tissue, postcards,
ribbon-wrapped and stinking of must.

He found the boat from Norway
that carried his grandfather to New York,
but knows nothing of the voyage.

His grandparents' marriage was duly recorded
in Michigan, as were the issue from that union,
but not what evenings were like at the dinner table.

He's translated the post cards from Grimstad,
his grandfather gone home to nurse his mother,
missing them, but nothing about why he stayed.

II.

On Mother's Day, we make the rounds
to visit our mothers and grandmothers
in Green-Wood, Evergreen, and Cypress Hills.

By his mother's stone, we picnic, warm our faces
in the spring sun as the kids play peek-a-boo
among the dead, try to scare us out of our wits.

He wants a picture. Me and the kids
by the oak that shades his mother in summer,
creaks and groans through winter.

Our son thinks he'll look better dangling from a branch,
shaking it free of withered leaves before landing hard
in the gnarled roots that cradle him like a baby.

Better, I think, to tell them a story to remember her.

Ossuaries

In Greece, where arable land is scarce
and cremation a sin, they dig up their dead
after three years, wash the bones in wine,
say the ritual prayers, file them in boxes
in the *koxalothoxion,* the bone-house.

The Choctaw leave their dead
to the elements on covered platforms
before sending in the bone pickers, tattooed
in honor of their work, who gather the bones,
use their long-nailed fingers to pick them clean.

In the Czech ossuary of Sedlec, a chandelier
of bone lights the nave, garlands of skulls
festoon vaulted arches, the handiwork
of crafty monks honoring the congregants
who rested briefly in soil from the Holy Land.

In Cologne, bone mosaics in cross-hatch patterns
adorn the walls of the Golden Chamber,
the reliquary of St. Ursula and her 11,000 virgins
slaughtered by the Huns, whose supplicants wrote
across the field of bone: "Holy Ursula, Pray for Us."

As Paris grew, they dug up their dead,
stacked their crisscrossed femurs,
skulls cheek to cheek, sorted by cemetery,
and for a small fee, you can visit them
in the catacombs under the suburban sprawl.

When my son was small, he asked
to be left in a cave when he died
so animals could come and feast
and when they were done,
they would scatter his bones in the forest.

I will return to nature, he told me, bright-eyed
at the prospect, as the mother in me thought *no*—
I will gather your bones, wash them in wine,
pick them clean, adorn the walls
with your lovely, long femurs, fashion mosaics
with the fine bones of your hands and feet.

I would build him an ossuary, keep him close,
but my hands cupping his skull, his shorn hair,
his face shining proudly only inches from mine—
I thought better of it, praised instead his wisdom,
how great his place in the world, his generous spirit.

The Perspective from Blue Bridge

I hope to one day let people see what i see.
    —Tyre D. Nichols, Photographer

> *Bridges perform*
> *an effective communication*
> *between two destinations.*

He is standing
before the arc of the bridge,
his camera low enough
to capture the curved spine
of brown bowed planks
warming in the afternoon sun,
the rails a bright cerulean blue,
his path to sage-colored trees
and cool shade unobstructed.

> *Standpoint: a position*
> *or perspective*
> *from which something*
> *is considered or evaluated.*

He is now the subject,
dragged from his car,
face down on the ground,
and as he tries
to calm them, says, *Okay,*
okay. I'm just trying
to go home,

the third eye mounted
on the officer's chest
records without consideration
for composition,
or any consideration at all.

> *Standpoint: a set of beliefs*
> *and ideas from which opinions*
> *and decisions are formed.*

Shot in black and white
among shadows
and streetlights,
there's no justification,
just the taser,
the pepper spray,
the boot 1-2-3 times
to his head,
the baton hammering
his back,
the fists to his face,
and each time he slumps over
no way to right himself.

> *Perspective: the capacity*
> *to view things in their true*
> *relations or relative importance.*

It's all about perspective,
whose point of view.
How else to explain
being out at sunset
to photograph
the waning light
and not make it home.
How else to explain
the threat of his desire
to live, to share
his vision.

> *Consider the bridge a pathway*
> *between two cultures, perhaps*
> *the bridge from war to peace.*

He was standing
before the arc of the bridge,
an aspiring photographer,
his camera low enough
to capture the curved spine
of brown bowed planks
warming in the afternoon sun,
with a story to tell,
the rails a bright cerulean blue,
his path to sage-colored trees
and cool shade unobstructed,
inviting us to see what he saw,

a bridge to cross—or not,
trees waiting in welcome,
the magnificent light
and landscape beckoning.

Detritus at the US-Mexican Border

Quarterly, archaeologists gather just south of the border
to map and photograph effects strewn across the desert.
No ancient Roman ruin a farmer stumbled upon
with his plow, here there's been no time for silting.
They mine the surface migrants slog across hoping
for better. When JFK was president and men walked
on the moon, archeologists found cocktail dresses,
high heels, indicators of migrant aspirations
for a life to be lived. Now it's a field scattered
with the detritus of survival, water bottles, lanterns,
those crinkly thermal blankets, light and warm
enough for the cold in outer space.

Citizens of Paradise:
Jay Austin and Lauren Geoghegan

*Grant me the desired homeland for which I long,
making me again a citizen of Paradise.*
— Greek Orthodox Liturgy

Circumnavigating this *great big beautiful world,*
an adventure on bicycles, full of love for each other,
for a world full of kindness, the Kazakh man
who gave them ice cream, the girls in Kyrgyzstan
who met them with flowers, hearths and hearts
open in welcome, you would have to hope
when the passing car filled with Tajikistani boy martyrs
turned, the young lovers never saw what came after,
you would have to hope not even a car full of militant boys
or their own mangled bikes and bodies, could stop their belief
people are *generous and wonderful and kind.*

What Heather Heyer's Mom Wants

Charlottesville was a little peanut . . . and the hate wasn't the kind of hate that you have here.
—Donald Trump on Pro-Palestinian protests.

The Charlottesville rally was so insignificant,
he chose to compare it to a little peanut, you know,
the legume African slaves brought with them,
planted all over the South, that nourished the poor.
He made clear in Charlottesville hate was different,
not vicious, more the lamentation for a lost culture
where everyone knew their place. He forgot,
it seems, the Neo-Nazis and white supremacists,
torches in hand, barking that Jews will not replace them.
He never mentions Heather Heyer, who lost her life
that day *some fine people* marched, or her mother
who wants us to know it's not about her daughter,
a white girl mowed down protesting for civil rights.
It's not about Heather's fear for America,
her empathy for others. Her mother knows
We've got a hate problem here, a hate so strong
you can fuel a car with it and no one's paying
attention. *The festering boil of hate has to be lanced,*
she says, the wound kept open, cleaned, attention paid.
She wants us to brace for the pain of healing.

Queers

Every family had an Aunt Georgette,
high-heeled, beehived, and cat-eyed,
and her *special friend,* Sally,
who favored sensible shoes,

along with a *confirmed bachelor* uncle,
Hal, who gave the best birthday presents,
phonographs and transistor radios,
and kept his friends to himself.

You wondered why
Aunt Georgette and Sally
were roommates at sixty,
how Uncle Hal stayed single
despite all the women
Grandma brought to his door,

but enlightenment came, following
Uncle Hal up the street, watching
his graceful arms, the swish of his hips,
like the first naming of things:
cup, spoon, cat—*queer.*

And just as quickly, there they were—
at weddings, baby showers, christenings,
the milestones others celebrate,
watching from the margins,

Aunt Georgette and Sally, *queers,*
Uncle Hal, *queer,*
cousins Jim, Chris, and Marlene, *queers!*

How quickly you, too, learned to code
in euphemism, the language of grownups
for people, more than you could ever imagine,
brave enough not to try it the other way,
to just live a *quiet* life with a *special friend*
who will appear in the obituary
as a *lifelong companion.*

The Pillars of Evolution

for Harriet Martineau

Darwin's Arch, a rock formation southeast of Darwin Island in the Galapagos archipelago, collapsed due to natural erosion.
—Ecuador Environment Ministry

I. Darwin's Arch

A question took Darwin to the Galapagos,
to an arch rough and barren,
where finches answered: beaks thick or sharp
favoring seed or flower, blood of seabirds,
each to his own niche illustrated how
from one ancestral finch, ground-dwelling,
seed eating, came adaptive radiation,
a result of supply and demand, the abundance
at a given time of cacti or insects,
survival of the fittest the ability to adapt,
take what is available, adjust accordingly.

II. The Descent of Man

A very Victorian Darwin discovered
a *wonderful woman,* a cigar smoking
journalist and sociologist, who extolled
education for women, the fiscal frailty
of slavery, its abhorrent nature,
earned her own keep and dazzled
a novice Darwin with her enterprise
while he nonetheless concluded
the second sex intellectually inferior
unless they, too, could become breadwinners,
and lamented the impact of such a departure
on the happiness of all their homes.
Who would care for the young, see to their needs?
Each, he concluded, belong in their own niche.

III. The Pillars of Evolution

Darwin's Arch, while commanding, was still
vulnerable to geologic time, a natural process
so slow, the inevitable collapse took its time,
arrived precisely at 11:20 a.m., a wonder
captured by tourists aboard the Aggressor III,
and as the waters now thread the remaining
pillars, birds still feed, and that second sex,
the one that foraged for berries, farmed
to feed her young, kept the fires burning
while men hunted for elusive game,
the adaptable second sex now stands
on her on her own, can face that other pillar,
and together, perhaps, they might evolve
side-by-side, witness to the fate of us all.

Branding

The interrogation of language requires your presence
at the table, knife and fork in hand, ready to feast
on savory pancakes smothered in Aunt Jemima's syrup.
And you need to know an Italian-American vaudevillian
in blackface birthed everyone's favorite mammy on stage,
her Aunt Jemima archetype and model for Nancy Green,
former slave, first trademark-in-the-flesh Aunt Jemima
flipping flapjacks at the Chicago World's Fair.

There needs to be an appreciation of just how many women
kept the trope going: Lillian Richard made an *honest* living,
put Hawkins, the *Pancake Capitol of Texas,* on the map.
Anna Robinson claimed *Only wif my magic recipe
can you turn out dese tender, 'licious, jiffy-quick pancakes.*
Rosa Washington Riles, a personal cook for corporate,
obliged her boss by donning the apron,
and Anna Short Harrington earned enough
to feed her children, buy a boarding house.

Here was the American dream at work, heads wrapped
in red and white kerchiefs, their aprons spotless.

Jazz singer Edith Wilson tried to dignify her
Aunt Jemima on TV and Ethel Ernestine Harper,
first Black teacher of history in Morristown, NJ,
ditched the kerchief for pearl earrings and a necklace.

The last "living" trademarked Aunt Jemima,
Rosie Lee Moore Hall, was just that, the last,
until Aylene Lewis, a friend of Walt's, served children
those 'licious pancakes as Mickey and Donald watched.

What could be wrong with that?

What could be wrong with women
able to turn the trope, make it work for them?
You would have to ask yourself, can you discern
the sweet from the bitter, not take offense
when Quaker Oats Corporate refused
to make a donation to mark Nancy Green's grave,
claimed their Aunt Jemima a fictional trademark,
no relation to Nancy Green at all.

Can you discard the rotten, reason
when you are full, satisfied,
know when enough is enough?

The Last Supper

After the narrative china paintings of Julie Green

California, 27 September 1929.
Hearty Breakfast.

He was only 15. 23 July 1947.
Fried Chicken Watermelon.

Louisiana, 07 January 2010.
Fried sac-a-lait fish, topped with crawfish etouffee,
a peanut butter and apple jelly sandwich
and chocolate chip cookies.

A chronicle of last suppers on porcelain in cobalt blue,
walls lined with plates no one will ever eat from,
mop up a rich gravy with a hunk of bread,
mash potatoes with the tines of a fork.

Put to you as a question: what would you like
for your last supper? Anything within reason.
What will it be? Something just for you, only you.

A cruel choice, perhaps, put to you as a reminder
of what's been lost, as you ask for your mother,
brought in special, to make her chicken dumplings,

or what's never been yours, the surprise
of your first birthday cake, a gift from the guards,

or the whimsey of a glass of Dom Perignon,
a jar of dill pickles, four olives, a steak
cut into cubes and puzzled back together.

Shall it be savory or sweet, that last taste on your tongue?

Your voracious desire evident in "Three fried chicken
thighs, 10 or 15 shrimp, tater tots with ketchup,
two slices of pecan pie, strawberry ice cream,
honey and biscuits, and a Coke,"

but no way to tell whether that last meal satisfied,
whether someone washed your feet, forgave you,
that others felt better having first fed you, joined you
for that last meal, then walked you down the long hall.

Imagine the possibilities reduced to a glass
of iced water, an apple, or simply nothing at all.

At the Bird Feeder

The wild French lilac
below the feeder serves
as a waiting room
for the patient sparrows and wrens,
Mr. & Mrs. Downy Woodpecker,
the clumsy blue jay
pumping wildly
to keep his perch,
each waiting their turn,
some happy enough with scraps,
the fallen sunflower seeds
that land on the porch,
no one claiming
a particular order,
although the palm-sized
house finches in their dusty red aprons
are usually the first,
the flashy jays and cardinals last.
For all the flitting branch to branch,
the quick swoops and darting
arrivals and departures,
they are a patient lot,
a diverse lot that appears
not to notice
what sets them apart,
focused as they are
on what brings them together.

Ibis

They get along with the spoonbills
and herons they nest beside,
so we think them a fine kettle of fish
—and understand the metaphor,
because Thoth, the ibis-headed
man-god, made words, so we can
understand. With his ibis head
he thought, and with his man body
he made the universe, did the math,
mouthed the words to describe
that which he wrought, balanced
good and evil, bound the human and divine,
surveyed the land, took up the plants
and healed the sick, mapped the stars
and wrote songs about them.
But these birds, with their ibis heads
and ibis bodies, do not take
to all that busyness, do not need
to broker swells for their supper,
are satisfied when mud will do.

Alchemy

To conjure my mother I get the milk,
sugar, rice, freshly ground cinnamon,
eggs, and I make her rice pudding.

Her directions, in award-winning
Palmer penmanship, indicate how
much and when, and a postscript—
we do not use raisins, *no raisins.*

This is where she now lives,
in her annotated church cookbook,
generations of women
whose recipes have come together,
overlaid by those of my mother.

Cooking must be the very first
chemistry, when someone thought
to put water with grain,
to sear a piece of meat,
to set a kettle on the fire.

And true alchemy wasn't turning
base metal to gold but rather
grapes into wine, hops into beer,
love into something to sustain us.

It's everything to do with the senses,
fragrant cinnamon on my fingertips,
my mother's capable hands stirring
rice and milk, right here at my stove,
insisting I get it right, then the spoon
raised as she beckons me, *taste.*

How to Eat at a Civilized Table

Be prepared to sit on the floor, perhaps on a pillow,
wipe your hands with a warm cloth,
pick and scoop your food with a pair of sticks.
Eat with the small end of the stick, serve with the larger.
Rest chopsticks on your plate and never across a rice bowl.

Elsewhere, be mindful to use your hands to eat,
and in some places, only the right hand
(the one without sin) to bring a tasty morsel to your lips.
There might be common bowls from which to share.
Understand, you will be expected to eat several servings.
To pass food to another, use only your right hand,
but be sure to pass to your left.

Seated at a formal table, a variety of utensils set before you,
work your way outward inward, upward downward,
keep the napkin on your lap, dab discreetly when necessary.
Note the names on the cards of those around you.
Banter when appropriate. Keep your hands above the table,
wrists gently set beside your plate, elbows off.

In all cases, humility and thankfulness are expected.

A Tale of Two Falafels

> *... a lesson in diplomacy. Mamoun has Arabs and Jews sitting at the same table.*
> —The Village Voice, 1976

Mamoun's Falafel and The Olive Tree Café sit
side by side, Arab and Israeli, on MacDougal St.

They both serve falafels and shawarma,
kebobs and ganouj, tahineh and tabbouleh.

How much sweeter it is to sit together
at a table laden with food, no matter whose,

than at tables with translators and
peacekeepers, negotiators and troublemakers.

Let us argue all day about whose *teta* or *safta*
made the best hummus, whose sweets are sweeter.

Better to wave broken bits of bread at one another
to exclaim our differences and then savor them.

A Family Outing in Harriman State Park

At Lake Askoti, stream-fed, well-stocked
with trout, bass, panfish, and fishers
skimming along in wooden canoes,
children wander to and from the water's edge,
dazzled by a dragonfly, a Muslim family,
women in hijabs and long dresses
looking cool despite the heat, lounge on benches,
while a Hasidim family pose their children
for pictures on an outcropping rock.
All take in the same mountain air, sweetness
they will carry down the mountain
in their lungs, their bones, their smiles,
the Muslim grandpa making silly faces
for the little Jewish girl with a shy smile.

In the Dark of Night

I.
Fresh from the womb-dark,
children rail against such blinding
blackness, fists madly pumping,
eyes hungry for what daylight brings,

while the old, having seen
enough, can appreciate the dark,
what surrender will bring,
welcome, even, the buzzing of a fly.

II.
Lights out, your mother says
and you are an invisible ninja,
stealthy in the inky black night,
the magic of feeling your hand

but not seeing it—a leap of faith,
what you know is there, what is not.
Under the cover of dark,
you can't get any braver than that.

III.
No wonder teenagers love
vampires. Lusting after
mayhem in the murky dark,
they forgo parents,

finding familiars in alleys
darker still, navigating
wine and blunts and sex
and their own bleak hearts.

IV.

With all that ambient light leaking
from digital clocks, the stereo,
the refrigerator, the microwave,
night isn't so dark anymore.

From space we must never look
dark enough, molten light
mapping our progress across
the plains and the mountains.

V.
I miss the night that blinds,
the sleep unconscious, hunkered
in the downy bed, night without
illumination, without dreams,

and the pleasure of birdsong
in the morning, my limbs
returned to me one by one,
me, awake for the first time.

Yes, I Talk Too Much

I talk too much. A problem
I recognize on people's faces,
that little bit into whatever it is
I'm telling them, eyes glazed
by a sudden arctic frost, the body
eerily immobile, faces fixed
as though any movement
might prolong the narrative,
expound their agony.

Sometimes, they look up
like martyred saints
awaiting the outstretched hand
of a heavenly savior
until their eyes brimming
with sorrow gaze downward,
their posture now penitent,
necks awaiting the sword
of true martyrdom.
Salvation, they realize,
will not come easily,
death a relief and a reward
if only I would just shut up—
shut up shut up shut up.

I want to make them happy,
of course I do,
but a narrative needs
detailed and polished silver
on a table set just so, so we arrive
at an end satisfying in its conclusion.

My poor husband has tried
to prod me along. Is there point?
Where is this going? Will I need
to know all of that? *Everything*
is the point, I tell him.
But he doesn't appreciate
a long drive without a map or GPS,
the discoveries
he might make along the way,
and it doesn't help his relief,
finally, my point
beautifully plated and served,
he's a hostage, after all, at the end
of detainment, finally set free,
not sure how that happened.

Sometimes I'm so engaged
by what people tell me,
I want to shout *me too, me too,*
every nerve in my face twitching
with shared excitement,
antsy as a five-year-old
told to sit still,
knowing it's rude not to,
but it's hard (ask any child)
and just like that,
a dam bursts, words streaming
along the embankment,
shearing trees, unmooring houses,
faces resigned to the fact
I just can't shut up.

Still, I need to learn
the art of quiet, appear
to listen attentively
with a beatific smile, face tipped
slightly, as though
beckoning with my good ear.
I don't understand why
I can't do that and talk
simultaneously,
the call and response
of sparrows,
but I do know my silence
would be welcome,
the way a person's
newfound intelligence
would be welcomed,
or their ability to rise up and walk,
see, hear, remember.
The point, the point is—it's hard
to control this mouth-brain of mine,
the incessant chirping, the excitement
of song that sparks song
to say here we are, alive and well.
But please, feel free to interrupt,
stick in your two cents' worth.
I welcome all the change
you have to offer.

Soft Power

A gift really, to get someone to want
what you want, to make attractive
the unimaginable, so appetizing,
they won't notice the sleight
of hand, a desire so seemingly new,
they'll marvel, head bent to whatever
it was you had planned for them all along,
eating out of the palm of your hand.

About the Author

Anne Sandor was born and raised in Brooklyn, New York. She holds a BA from Vassar College and an MFA from Vermont College. A poet and fiction writer, her work has appeared in numerous publications. Her poem, "The Last Supper," appeared in the anthology, *Strange Fruit: Poems on the Death Penalty.* Most recently, her flash fiction story, "A Spare Kidney," and poem, "The Perspective from Blue Bridge," were *New Millenium* Awards Honorable Mentions. Her poem, "Mirror Writing," received an Honorable Mention in the 2024 Allen Ginsberg Poetry Awards.

Website:
www.annesandor.com

www.ingramcontent.com/pod-product-compliance
Lightning Source LLC
Chambersburg PA
CBHW031205160426
43193CB00008B/504